Old Dalbeattie and Palnackie
Bernard Byrom

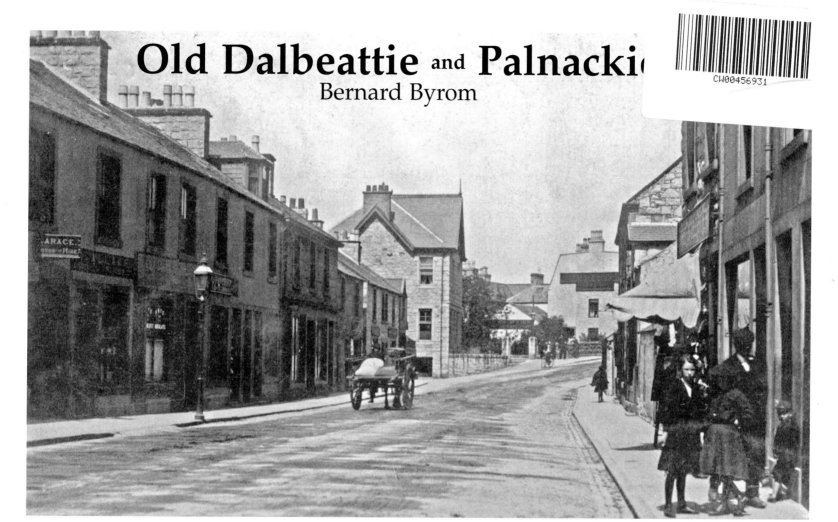

The High Street runs from Maxwell Street down the side of the town hall in a generally southerly direction. In this1908 scene a horse pulling a delivery cart is trudging northwards along it and approaching the new post office on the left; beyond it over the bridge across the Dalbeattie Burn is the side of the Commercial Hotel. The writing is already literally on the wall for this mode of transport because the sign belonging to the Crown Hotel on the left side of the street is advertising a garage with motors for hire. The cart is passing what are now the premises of Bowmans chemists with its three upstairs windows and two large shop-front windows; the shop immediately to the right of the lamp post is now M Corson, bakers, and the De-Caff café is to its left.

© Bernard Byrom, 2010
First published in the United Kingdom, 2010,
by Stenlake Publishing Ltd.
www.stenlake.co.uk

ISBN 9781840334937

This bridge in the High Street over the Dalbeattie Burn was built sometime shortly before 1850, was widened in 1860 and again in 1930 when it acquired its granite balustrades. Before the bridge was built the burn had to be crossed by a ford with stepping stones at Islesteps, at the end of Water Street, and the road continued from there into the end of Mill Street. The stepping stones have since been replaced by a footbridge close to the town hall car park from where a footpath leads to Mill Street. The building in the centre of the picture, which is on the far side of the bridge, is part of the town hall; on the nearside of the bridge are the former Commercial Hotel (nowadays the Pheasant Hotel) on the left and the back of the post office is on the right.

Introduction

The town of Dalbeattie (Gaelic: *Dail Bheithe*, "Valley of the Birch Trees") lies in the Stewartry of Kirkcudbright about fifteen miles south-west of Dumfries. In 1372 Archibald the Grim, son of Sir James Douglas "the Good", became Lord of Galloway and appointed a steward to collect his revenues and administer justice, hence Kirkcudbrightshire became known as a Stewartry rather than a county. In 1975 the ancient Stewartry of Kirkcudbright was abolished and both Dalbeattie and Palnackie became part of the Dumfries & Galloway Region.

Dalbeattie is situated on the east bank of the River Urr about five miles from its mouth on the estuary of the Solway Firth. Since the Middle Ages it has straddled the Dalbeattie Burn, the settlement on the northern side at that time being known as Meikle Dalbeattie and the one on the southern side as Little Dalbeattie. Around 1780 the land on both sides of the Burn was feued, that part on the north by Mr George Maxwell of Munches and that on the south by Mr Alexander Copland of Kingsgrange. Each feuar was granted a plot of land for a house and garden, an allotment for perpetuity and the right to cut peat turves on Aucheninnes Moss above Barrhill, this latter facility being necessary because of the heavy tax payable upon coals that had to be imported from England. These feus were quickly in great demand because the area was very desirable for development and, in consequence, the village grew rapidly. The soil was generally fertile, especially in the lower lands that lay round the valley of the Urr. Moreover the glacial erosion in the last ice age had carved out the valley of the Urr Water, exposing on both sides large outcrops of high quality granite. Although this had long been used locally as building material for walls and farm buildings it wasn't until around 1780 that it was first used for making millstones and 1810 before the first proper quarry was opened at Craignair. Granite then rapidly became recognised as ideal for public buildings and paving and it was not long before other quarries were opened in the locality. If Aberdeen is the Granite City, Dalbeattie must surely be the Granite Town because the majority of its older buildings (and many newer ones) are built of it.

The Dalbeattie Burn rises in the hills to the north-east and makes its circuitous way through the town with sufficient force to have enabled mills to be established along its banks. A grain mill existed from at least the mid 1600s and was joined in the following century by a lint mill and a papermaking mill. By the beginning of the nineteenth century the village was thriving; apart from the newly-established granite industry there were several farms in the area and agricultural prices were high because of the Napoleonic Wars. This gave the incentive to improve agricultural methods and to bring new land into cultivation which in turn created more jobs. The River Urr is tidal up to Dalbeattie so small-tonnage craft were able to bring imports, mainly of lime and coal, and to export grain and potatoes. These imports necessitated improvements to the local roads so that goods could be more easily transported up-country. One such road was built from Dalbeattie to Kirkpatrick-Durham and in 1800 a new turnpike road was opened from Dumfries to Castle Douglas, being extended to Portpatrick in 1807. This prosperity was too good to last. The ending of the Napoleonic Wars with France in 1815 caused a slump in the prices obtained for farm products and resulted in a long period of trade depression that, apart from a few good years in the 1830s, lasted almost to the middle of the century. By the 1840s there was a large Irish population in the area but there were not enough jobs so there was widespread poverty. The economy began to improve in the middle of the century and farm servants' wages doubled, but in the late 1880s economic depression began to set in again and this lasted for most of the next decade. In spite of this, agricultural improvements continued with turnips gradually displacing potatoes as the principal green crop and artificial manures being developed. Steamship services were developed to export local produce to places such as Liverpool and Glasgow, returning with lime from Cumberland and bone-meal from Liverpool whilst Dalbeattie granite began to be exported to many English towns and cities and even further afield. From the eighteenth century Dalbeattie had its own small port on the Dalbeattie Burn at the Dub O' Hass (which can be translated as the "pool at the throat of the river" or alternatively as the "hole in the bank") near its junction with the Urr. This harbour basin had been constructed sometime before the 1740s but by 1745 it was inadequate for the volume of shipping so a granite-faced 'New Quay' was erected about 200 yards south of the Dub O'Hass. The estuary of the Urr, known as Rough Firth, was navigable by ships of up to 100 tons and small vessels could ascend as far as the mouth of the Dalbeattie Burn, but the navigation channel is quite shallow and tortuous and ships had frequently to be poled up to the Dub O'Hass or drawn there by horses. There was for many years a shipbuilding industry in the vicinity which continued until the 1880s. The last ship to be built at Dalbeattie was the *Jane Elizabeth* but she was known throughout the area as "The Curse". This had nothing to do with her career; the story goes that at her launching the gentleman who was performing the naming ceremony accidentally dropped the bottle with which the christening should have been done and, instead of saying the name of the vessel, he uttered a hearty curse!

By 1825 there were an innkeeper and five publicans and spirit dealers in the town. This number was regarded by the Kirk Session as being far too many for such a small town. In 1829 and again in1830 they complained of excessive drinking and riotous behaviour. They were also concerned about the number and character of the lodging houses in the town, saying that they were largely occupied by sturdy beggars or vagrants of a dangerous type who infested the parish. In spite of these strictures, by 1837 there were seven hostelries in the town: the Brown Cow, the Commercial, the Copland Arms, the King's Arms, the Maxwell Arms, the Plough and the Thistle.

In 1835 the town consisted virtually of four streets: High Street, Copland Street, William Street and Maxwell Street. Work had been started on a few other streets but they hadn't yet been fully developed. More mills had been constructed; there were now also a waulk (woollen) mill, two sawmills and one engaged in bacon curing. Soon afterwards came Thomas Biggar with farm seeds and artificial manures and Messrs Helme who were wood merchants and bobbin turners. By this time a number of small vessels had been built at the Dub O'Hass and were plying between the village and the English coast. By 1850 there were many more streets in the town and it was reckoned there were around 300 inhabited dwellings housing around 1,500 inhabitants, with a corresponding increase in the number of trades and occupations.

Communications with the outside world had also been improved. Pigott & Co's Directory for 1825 shows that letters were taken from Dalbeattie every Monday, Wednesday and Saturday morning by John McNish at one penny each. He returned the same day bringing letters for Dalbeattie at three-halfpence each. Robert Adamson operated a carrier service to Dumfries every Wednesday and Saturday, returning the same day, and William Butter carried to Edinburgh every second Wednesday. There was also a service to Colvend on Tuesdays and Thursdays and to Auchencairn on Thursdays. By 1837 David Murray was the Dalbeattie postmaster and letters arrived daily from Castle Douglas at 3pm with a return service at 6pm. Anyone wanting to go to Carlisle and on to London had to go to Crossmichael for the coach, eastbound at 3pm and westwards at 6pm to Portpatrick. There was a stagecoach from the Maxwell Arms to Dumfries at 7pm daily except Sundays and to Kirkcudbright similarly at 11am. Slater's Directory for 1852 shows that there were two coaches (originating from Kirkcudbright) at 8am every morning to Dumfries and on the return journey to Kirkcudbright there was the Royal Mail coach from Dumfries at 10am and two coaches in the evening at 6pm. Only one carrier is listed: James Hyslop from Dalbeattie's Mill Street to Dumfries every Wednesday and Saturday. The Urr was served by two steamers, the *Countess of Selkirk* (built 1835) and the *Saint Andrew*, the latter providing a fortnightly service to Whitehaven and Liverpool for passengers and goods.

The second half of the nineteenth century saw considerable progress in the town's affairs. In 1858 Dalbeattie became a Police Burgh; its first police station was opened almost opposite the Maxwell Arms, but was later replaced by a police house in Station Road and then by the present police station in Craignair Street. In the following year the Dalbeattie Gas Light Company was formed and in November of that year the railway was extended from Dumfries to Castle Douglas via Dalbeattie. A gravity-fed water supply from the Buittle Hills was installed in 1879 and subsequently a mains sewerage system which helped to make Dalbeattie a relatively healthy place to live and work during the boom granite years of the 1880s. A branch of the Commercial Bank of Scotland opened in May 1889; this bank merged with the National Bank of Scotland in 1959 and the combined bank merged with the Royal Bank of Scotland in 1969. Between 1891 and 1902 the principal streets were paved and kerbed.

The early part of the twentieth century saw further progress with the first bus service on the Dumfries to Castle Douglas route being started in 1921 by James Dickson of Newbridge Farm, Dumfries. The "Guy" model of bus had solid tyres and its speed was limited to 12mph. It had an open top with a fold-down hood at the rear and held 25 passengers. Wartime industry included a large ammunition factory nearby at Edingham and several others not far away along the Solway The Edingham factory was set up by the Ministry of Supply, chiefly to make cordite for artillery and naval guns and it was constructed by gangs of Irish labourers who were lodged in timber barracks just outside Dalbeattie; their camp was later taken over to house German prisoners. After the war the factory was given over to munitions storage and bargeloads were often brought into Palnackie Harbour.

Unfortunately the second half of the century saw a decline in the region's industry. The railway between Dumfries and Stranraer via Dalbeattie and Castle Douglas was closed in 1965 as part of the "Beeching Axe" and in the same year the Royal Navy Armaments Depot decided to stop bringing bargeloads of munitions to Palnackie Basin and to use road transport to Edingham instead. By 1970 Dalbeattie had lost its cattle market, cheese factory, dairy, two quarries and a brickworks and by 1996 both of the feed mills had also closed. The paper mill started by the Coplands in 1793 closed in 1953. The town is nowadays home to around 4,500 people and is still the most important town in the Stewartry. Apart from granite and forest-based industries, tourism is one of its most important sources of income nowadays, but this is only seasonal. A major project at the present time is the restoration of the port at the Dub O'Hass. In the early years of the twentieth century there was still a thriving trade with exports to Liverpool and other north of England ports of granite and wood and imports of manures and feeding stuffs for cattle as well as rags for the paper mills, but the port has been unused since the mid-1960s and by the early years of the 21st century it had become overgrown and derelict. The site has recently been cleared by Dalbeattie Community Initiative and Phase 1 of the port restoration project was officially re-opened on 3rd August 2008 by Alex Fergusson MSP. Phase 2 will include restoration of the quayside walls.

The village and port of Palnackie is south of Buittle on the western side of the Urr about four miles from Dalbeattie. It lies on a creek on the opposite bank of the Urr to Dalbeattie and a little way downstream so it was able to handle larger ships than Dalbeattie. Its first recorded harbour was no more than a single wooden quay on one side of the river creek where up to six boats could moor. This quay was about 300 feet long with a maximum depth of water of twenty feet. By 1850 proper quays had been built on both sides of the creek, forming a basin 40 feet wide with the granite quays being reinforced by timber piling. At one time vessels of up to 350 tons burthen could load and unload cargo here but silting reduced this depth. Even so, ships of 300 tons burthen were still able to use the basin in the early 1900s. Around 120 to 130 vessels used to be discharged annually. About a quarter of these were steamers and the remainder sailing vessels, and their average carrying capacity was about 150 tons. Until the railway came Palnackie was

the outlet for Castle Douglas's exports. Between the 1940s and the mid-1960s ammunition barges used to unload here and as late as 1965 the Port Mill unloaded fertiliser at the quay. Pigott & Co's 1837 Directory shows there was a post office run by Thomas Dalling in the village with a daily foot service to Castle Douglas. The public houses were the Anchor (John Robson), Royal Oak (Thomas Dalling) and the Ship (William Candlish). There were also thirteen tradesmen and a schoolmaster. David McLune ran a carrier service to Dalbeattie every Thursday and a fortnightly service to Castle Douglas and Kirkcudbright, from where there was a connection to Glasgow. Nowadays Palnackie has a population of around 150, one shop/post office (the "Crow's Nest"), a primary school (built 1953), a pub and restaurant (the Glenisle Inn) and several businesses. Until recently the village hosted the Grande Internationale World Flounder Tramping Championships. Tramping is a traditional method in south west Scotland of catching flounder or other flat fish by wading in shallow water, feeling with the toes for flounder hiding in the mud and standing on them. At one time a leister (trident) was often used to impale the fish but this practice was discontinued for safety reasons. The competition began in 1972 and was held to raise funds for the Royal National Lifeboat Institution but has not been held since 2007 because of the increasingly large organisation needed to run the event and the high cost of insurance required to meet health and safety requirements.

Further Reading

The books listed below were used by the author during his research.

David Frew, *The Parish of Urr*, 1909, reprinted 1993.
John Gifford, *The Buildings of Scotland – Dumfries and Galloway*, 1996
Ian Donnachie, *The Industrial Archaeology of Galloway*, 1971
Rev C H Dick, *Highways & Byways in Galloway & Carrick*, reprinted 2001
Ruth & Leslie Morris, *Scottish Harbours: The Harbours of Mainland Scotland*, 1983
Ordnance Gazetteer of Scotland, 1882 - 1885

The Statistical Accounts of Scotland 1791-1799 and 1845
Pigott & Co's Directories, 1825 and 1837
Slater's Directory, 1852
Town & County Directory, 1938
Dalbeattie Town History website (editor Richard Edkins)
Dalbeattie Matters website

The interested reader is also recommended to visit the Dalbeattie Museum on the corner of High Street and Southwick Street where many old photographs and items connected with the history of the area are on display.

Acknowledgements

The author wishes to thank the following for their assistance during the research of this book:
Mr Tommy Henderson of Dalbeattie Museum, the staff of Dalbeattie Library and the Ewart Library in Dumfries and the many local people who volunteered information in the course of his field research.

Maxwell Street in the 1920s. John Street runs off to the left, Water Street is straight ahead and High Street begins its course between the town hall and the Commercial Hotel. On the extreme right of the picture is the Maxwell Arms, dating from the late 1790s and the oldest hotel in the town, and next to it is John M'Kie's Drapery Warehouse. This shop was originally opened in 1832 by Thomas Rowline who became a JP for the Stewartry and was one of the members of the first Police Commission after Dalbeattie became a burgh. He was also one of the original proprietors of the Dumfries & Galloway Standard newspaper. Beyond it is the Commercial Hotel whose clients in those days were principally commercial travellers. Both hotels have been considerably enlarged over the years and all three buildings have lost the bold lettering proclaiming their names. The Commercial Hotel, which is currently named the Pheasant Hotel, has also lost its portico and McKie's shop has lost its curved top.The building on the left dates from 1800 and was originally rectangular in shape. In the middle of the nineteenth century it was rebuilt into its present shape with a castellated top to show the versatility of granite as a building material and became known as the Round House. In this picture it is Gowin's Ladies and Gentlemen's Outfitters shop; nowadays it is the Dumfries & Galloway Canine Rescue Centre and the upper floor is a private flat. The motor garage to its left is now owned by J Paterson & Sons who sell all-terrain vehicles.

A 1962 photo of the town hall end of the High Street. By now the Commercial Hotel has become the Galloway Arms and the bridge over the Dalbeattie Burn is in the foreground. Opposite the hotel is the side of the town hall where a plaque on its wall commemorates the memory of Lieutenant William McMaster Murdoch, First Officer on RMS *Titanic*, who died on the night of 14th April 1912 when the ship struck an iceberg in the north Atlantic. He was a native of Dalbeattie and as well as this civic memorial being erected, his local school instituted a memorial prize in his honour. Straight ahead is the building on the corner of John Street and Station Road that was designed by William A Railton of Kilmarnock in 1856 for the Union Bank of Scotland. This bank was first established in Dalbeattie in 1852 when its office was opened in a shop on the west side of High Street, four doors up from the Cross and in 1858 it moved into this new building on what had been formerly known as "Jennie Robinson's field". The building was altered in 1877. In 1955 the Union Bank amalgamated with the Bank of Scotland and nowadays trades in Dalbeattie as HBOS from a small hutch of an office built onto the side of this handsome granite building.

Dalbeattie's post office in the High Street just below the bridge over the Dalbeattie Burn was designed by J A Macgregor in 1902-03 and this picture of it dates from 1912. The town's first postal service was run from a room in the Commercial Hotel by the manager and his wife and, at that time, it was only classed as a receiving and delivery office under the main office at Castle Douglas with a daily runner to and from that town. When the business outgrew the room at the hotel in the 1850s it was transferred to a house on the west side of the High Street just below the burn. From there it was subsequently moved to a house on the opposite side of the street from the Maxwell Arms, then moved yet again to the corner premises below the town clock before finally moving into its present home in 1903.

High Street, Dalbeattie

JV 60759

A 1908 view of the High Street looking south from near the post office towards the Cross. The buildings are mainly late 18th century and 19th century vernacular in their style and transport is pictured in both traditional and more modern modes. Approaching on the right appears to be a gentleman in a top hat driving himself in a pony and trap whilst on the left is a steam traction engine, the epitome of modern industry, hauling a cart and possibly carrying out road repairs.

The postmark on this postcard dated 16th August 1914 says it all. Twelve days earlier Great Britain had declared war on Germany and here we see Dalbeattie recruits, still wearing civilian clothes, parading in the High Street near the Cross and watched by an admiring crowd. They had enlisted in the local regiment, the 5th King's Own Scottish Borderers.

The area of the High Street at its junction with Mill Street is the focal point of the town and is known as the Cross. This Edwardian view is looking back from the Cross up the High Street with the new post office in the distance and, beyond it, the side of the Commercial Hotel. Back at the Cross, the premises on the left belong to D Newall, a chemist who had now branched out into photographic dealership, and next to him is the shop of D C Crosbie & Co, provision merchants. Across the road is the large and versatile shop of R Blythe whose merchandise ranged from furnishings to ironmongery. The memorial standing in front of the shop is Queen Victoria's Jubilee Fountain. Built of grey and pink granite and erected by D H & J Newall in 1887, it is inscribed on one side "Victoria Jubilee Memorial 1837 - 1887" and on the other side "Erected by Public Subscription". It is a fountain with a bowl for humans to drink on one side at elbow height and a space in the base for dogs; thirsty horses were catered for at a horse trough in Maxwell Street.

These buildings at the corner of High Street and Mill Street date from 1883. The shop on the corner was still occupied by R Blyth who appears to have given up the furnishing side of his business. The three-storey part with the iron-crested French-style tower and the buildings to the right stretching into Mill Street were a later addition and were built at a slight angle to the main street at the request of the local doctor who wished to have an unobstructed view into the High Street from his home at Alma House further up Mill Street.

HIGH STREET, DALBEATTIE.

This view is looking back towards the Cross from further down the High Street. Lindsay's Supply Stores on the left sold a range of groceries whilst Thomas Aitchison on the right was a fish, poultry and produce merchant.

The scene at the Cross in the 1930s when motor cars had largely replaced the horse-drawn carriages and carts. R Blyth have removed their premises to the newer part of the block and are once again advertising their services as furnishers, whilst most of their former premises have been taken over by the "Easiphit" shoe firm of Greenlees & Sons, R Hastings' stationers shop being squeezed between them. The new building in Mill Street is occupied by Messrs Brown & Carson's butchers shop which still trades today as TH Carson Traditional Family Butchers. The Kings Arms Hotel is on the right-hand side of the High Street, displaying an AA sign and with its garage's petrol pump standing on the pavement outside.

The large villa on the left of this 1909 view of Alpine Street is Anchor Mount which is completely unchanged today, but the small building opposite has had dormer windows added. This was the home of the five Henderson brothers who are standing next to the errand boy with his basket. The house at the foot of the hill (actually on Mill Street) is Alma House which was built for the local doctor in the mid-19th century with a projecting bay topped by an Italianate tower.

King Edward the Seventh succeeded to the throne in 1901 and his coronation was arranged to take place on 26th June 1902. Two days before the due date, the King was operated on for appendicitis and the coronation had to be postponed to 9th August. Similarly, events that had been planned in towns and villages all over Britain were postponed until the new date. In this picture the head of Dalbeattie's coronation procession is wending its way up High Street into Maxwell Street between the town hall on the left and the Commercial Hotel on the right.

The great and the good of Dalbeattie have assembled at the Cross to hear the provost make a proclamation. They are flanked on all sides by a line of soldiers with shouldered arms and a large crowd has gathered. But what is the event? From the appearance and headgear of the audience it may have been the official proclamation of King George the Fifth's accession to the throne in 1910.

Another procession through Dalbeattie, the display of flags suggesting that it may be celebrating the coronation of King George the Fifth which took place on 2nd June 1911. The cavalcade is making its way from John Street into Maxwell Street past the "Round House" which can be seen in the background with Water Street to its right. The floats represented the various trades associated with the town, the nearest one in the picture being that of the local blacksmiths. For centuries Dalbeattie also had an established fair day of its own which used to be celebrated twice a year. Crowds came from miles around and used to gather in the High Street as showmen and travelling merchants of all descriptions came to the town. Increasing industrialisation was probably the reason why these fairs were discontinued sometime around the 1860s.

In the early years of the twentieth century a group of female workers (attended by a few young men) are taking a break outside the glove factory that once existed in the High Street and lasted until at least the end of the First World War. The gloves worn by Captain Scott and his party on their last expedition to the South Pole were made here. The factory afterwards became the premises of McCubbin's the Saddlers and during the Second World War was used as a canteen and billet before subsequently reopening. It had a number of different owners but when its final owner, Kastix Ltd. went into receivership in 2001 it closed for good. The factory was situated a few yards north of the present Costcutter shop; its buildings and the adjoining house were demolished and a block of five flats built in its place on High Street. Behind these flats, where the factory used to extend backwards, a housing association complex called Loreburn has been built in its place.

A pre-First World War photograph of part of the interior of the glove factory. Apart from the light coming through the large windows, lighting was provided by electric lights suspended from the roof. The machines and stools for the all-female workforce are placed very close together and working conditions must have been very cramped but were probably quite good by the standards of many factories of the time. The girls themselves look healthy and well-nourished, a great contrast to similar contemporary photographs taken in factories in the big industrial towns and cities.

This is a picture of Port Street which runs from the lower end of the High Street down to the old port of Dalbeattie at the Dub O' Hass. The nearest buildings on the right were a side entrance to the glove factory in the High Street; they were demolished and replaced by the driveway to the apartment blocks in McArdle Place. The next house is still there although its pointed dormers have been replaced by modern ones, but the houses immediately beyond it have been demolished and replaced by new houses. Beyond them the opening on the right has been made into Glenshalloch Road which runs parallel to the High Street and contains modern housing.

Dalbeattie Harbour basin is at the Dub O' Hass on the east bank of the River Urr just south of its confluence with the Dalbeattie Burn. Its granite quays were laid down in the eighteenth century and a regular trade was maintained between the town and ports on the English side of the Solway Firth as far south as Liverpool. Exports over the years mainly consisted of granite and wood whilst imports were principally of coal, fertilisers, cattle feed and rags for the Dalbeattie paper mills. The port could only accommodate small ships, slightly larger ones using the port of Palnackie on the opposite side of the River Urr. By the 1960s Dalbeattie had become uneconomic as a port. The quayside subsequently became overgrown and totally derelict but thanks to the efforts of the Dalbeattie Community Initiative the port is currently being renovated and restored.

This is Station Road where Dalbeattie's second police station was built; it is the taller house at the end of the second terrace on the left. Its outhouses behind the house used to be the cells and still have bars on the windows (albeit a reconstruction within modern windows) and a false chimney stack was built that supported an air raid siren in the 1940s. Today the road looks very similar. The nearest house on the right in the block called Craigland was once the home of Dr. Gemmell, who built a surgery onto the side, and is is now the premises of The Bard Veterinary Group.

The Castle Douglas & Dumfries Railway Company was formed in March 1857 with WH Maxwell of Munches as its Chairman. The first survey of the line had been carried out in 1853 but the Parliamentary Bill didn't receive the Royal assent until July 1856. The line was 19 miles long, its engineer was Andrew Galloway and the capital raised was £187,785, half of which was subscribed by the much larger Glasgow & South Western Railway who absorbed the line on 5th July 1865. A great dinner party for more than 70 guests was held on 18th October 1859 at the Commercial Hotel to celebrate the opening of the line, with a procession from the station headed by the Dumfriesshire Militia and a firework display at night. Two years later the line was extended to Portpatrick and Stranraer from where ferries sailed to Larne in Northern Ireland. The route acquired the nickname of "The Port Road" and the boat trains were referred to as "The Paddy". The line was initially single track but in 1876 it was doubled as far as Lochanhead, then to Southwick by March 1878 and to Castle Douglas in 1880 with a new viaduct being constructed over the River Urr. The town's trade and industry were greatly increased with the coming of the railway but the twentieth century brought increasing competition from road haulage. A victm of Beeching, the line was closed between Dumfries and Challoch Junction on 14th June 1965, the boat trains being diverted from Dumfries to reach Stranraer via Kilmarnock and Ayr. In this picture a westbound train for Stranraer is entering Dalbeattie Station from the Dumfries direction. Practically nothing at all now remains of this attractive little station except for a small section of the eastbound platform.

St Peter's Roman Catholic Church is the oldest church in Dalbeattie. In spite of severe penalties meted out to Catholics over the centuries the old religion never completely died out in the area. This was helped by the fact that George Maxwell, a judge-ordinary of the county and a highly respected man locally, was the proprietor of Munches between 1637 and 1683. The authorities knew very well that he was a Catholic but because he went about practising his religion discreetly they left him in peace. This enabled him to use a part of his house as a chapel and Catholics from all over the area used to secretly attend services there. At the time of the Old Statistical Account in 1794 there were only 28 Catholic families recorded in the parish, but the early years of the nineteenth century saw an influx of Irish families which led to this church being built in 1814 with a school and presbytery adjacent. The land was provided by the then proprietor of Munches and the church was built of pink granite with red sandstone dressings. The grey granite tower and spire were added around 1850 but the spire was removed some years ago.

St. Peter's, Dalbeattie.

The first Church of Scotland church in Dalbeattie was the former Cameronian church in Burn Street which was purchased from them in 1842 and improved to accommodate 500 worshippers. Many of these worshippers were lost to the Free Church at the Disruption in the following year but by the late 1870s their numbers had recovered with the expansion of the town and more spacious accommodation was needed. In 1878 Mr Wellwood Herries Maxwell of Munches gifted a site for this new church in Craignair Street. His wife laid its foundation stone on 24th December that year and the building was opened for worship on 27th January 1880. It was designed by the Edinburgh architects, Messrs Kinnear & Peddie and was built of granite in Gothic cruciform style with accommodation for 850 worshippers. Its total cost was £3,876 exclusive of the spire which was paid for by Mr Maxwell himself. This picture dates from around the time of the First World War.

In the middle of the nineteenth century the Dalbeattie Burn was diverted to a new course so that it could provide power for corn and saw mills. The area between the old and new courses was cleared of vegetation and the town's bowling green was laid out on it sometime after 1860. A photograph taken of the bowling green in the 1890s shows many players wearing morning coats and top hats as they bowled. This picture dates from 1908 and the stone building on the right is the former Church of Scotland Hall of 1880 on Burn Street. The bowling green still flourishes today, although a new pavilion has been built around the one shown here. The church hall, which is nowadays the Dalbeattie Day Centre, is still recognisable although the windows visible in the picture have been removed.

With the original Free Church of 1843 (nowadays the Park Baptist Church) in the background of this 1888 picture the Dalbeattie Burn is winding its way through the town past an artificial lake created in a corner of Colliston Park. The stepping stones in the distance are close to the ford that was once the only way of crossing the burn in the town centre area before the bridge in the High Street was constructed around 1850. They were replaced by a footbridge in the late 1970s. The houses on the right are on John Street which runs parallel to the burn at this point.

This is a 1913 view of John Street with the United Presbyterian Church of 1861, designed by James Barbour of Dumfries, on the left and its manse, built by Robert Baldie in 1872, next door. The Free Church had an extremely chequered career in Scotland. The first secession from the Church of Scotland occurred in 1733 but the Secessionists themselves soon began arguing amongst themselves and split into further splinter groups. Many of these Free Churches eventually made up their differences and in 1847 formed themselves into the United Presbyterian Church. They in turn re-united with the Church of Scotland in 1929 and this church became redundant. For a time it became the Colliston Boys Club but was converted into private flats in the 1990s and is called Blair House. The row of granite-walled cottages to the right are of late 19th century construction.

Colliston Park was a gift to the burgh by Mrs Copland of Colliston in 1900 and covers ten acres of land. In 1906 Mr WJH Maxwell of Munches presented an adjoining piece of ground, formerly known as "Daniel", which was where the Dalbeattie Cricket Club played their matches and is now the location of the youth club. This area became known as the Munches Park and because it was on the other side of the Dalbeattie Burn it was linked to Colliston Park by a footbridge. Both parks were formally opened on 18th July 1908 at the conclusion of a day of events and ceremonies that included a grand procession to mark the 50th anniversary of Dalbeattie becoming a police burgh. Both of these events were celebrated a century later during 2008 by a programme of events in the park and the installation of new children's play equipment. The lattice bridge that connects John Street with the park was constructed in 1902 by the local firm of Robert Erskine. This view of the park dates from 1927 at the time when a field gun from the First World War was displayed by the lakeside. Unfortunately, the gun didn't survive the Second World War and was melted down for scrap iron.

A 1909 view of the octagonal bandstand that was erected in Colliston Park in 1900 and is now a Grade "B" listed structure that was refurbished in 2006. It was built by a local man, James Maxwell Wilson, and its cast iron columns were former gas streetlight pillars manufactured by the Lion Foundry at Kirkintilloch that were bought from Glasgow Corporation when electric street lighting was introduced into that city. John Street is in the background with the former United Presbyterian Church visible on the left.

IN MEMORIAM
OUR GLORIOUS DEAD
1914-1918.

Dalbeattie War Memorial.

The war memorial in Colliston Park was unveiled on Sunday 4th September 1921 by William Duncan Alexander who had been blinded a few years earlier whilst serving with the Royal Scots Fusiliers at Vimy Ridge during the First World War. Many regiments are represented on the memorial but the majority of soldiers are from the King's Own Scottish Borderers. The granite memorial's design is a simplified version of the Edinburgh Mercat Cross with the octagonal drum base supporting a column topped by the lion rampant of Galloway. The first wreath-laying ceremony took place on Remembrance Day in 1921.

Spycraig Hill, from which this photograph was taken, overlooks the town, and is situated just to the north of Aucheninnes Woods. It features in the area's smuggling history because it was here that lookouts were stationed to watch for Gaugers, the Revenue men who tried to halt smuggling from Sandyhills inland along what is now Moss Road past Barend. The house in the foreground stands end on to Spycraig Road which, beyond the gate on the left, becomes a footpath through the woods. The nearer row of houses running across the picture is on Southwick Road. Judging from the amount of smoke coming from their chimneys the day of the photograph must have been cold and windy. The further row of houses are those on Alpine Street, with the spire of the former Free Church (the present day Park Baptist Church) to the left. In the distance the smoke billowing over the town is coming from the Craignair Quarry.

This bridge at Barrhill used to be the lowest bridge across the Dalbeattie Burn until the High Street bridge was built shortly before 1850. Near this point the burn flows quite rapidly and this enabled local businesses to utilise its power to drive their mills, the water for this being diverted through the left hand arch on the bridge. One of these mills, which was in business by the 1830s, was the Mill Forge with water power driving the blacksmith's bellows and, later, his trip-hammer. Another was a small cattle feed mill that grew in time to become Carswell's Mill. The building in the picture is the east block of the Public School that was added in 1900.

Barrhill, Dalbeattie

This 1913 photograph shows Southwick Road crossing the Dalbeattie Burn and running up into Barrhill. Carswell's Mill's new warehouse is on the right with sacks of flour being loaded from a first-floor loading platform onto a cart whilst an elderly and a young villager watch the fast-flowing waters below the bridge. The large house in the picture belonged to the Carswell mill-owning family and the terrace of houses beyond it on Barrhill Road were known as "Sunnyside". William McMaster Murdoch who was the First Officer on board the liner *Titanic* was born in No. 3 in 1873. In early days, when Dalbeattie was still a small village, this area was a separate small village called Cunningham. Today no trace remains of the warehouse, but all the houses are still intact.

A panoramic view looking across the town to Barrhill in 1933. The former Public School is prominent in the picture and to the left of it are the buildings of Carswell's Mill. Behind them is Barrhill Road which runs to the left from the Sunnyside cottages down to its eventual junction with John Street. The course of the Dalbeattie Burn is marked by the curving line of trees past Colliston Park whose hexagonal bandstand roof can just be made out above the house on the right.

These substantial villas on Barrhill Road are arguably the best-situated houses in the town, being built on a south and south-westerly-facing hillside with a panoramic view over Dalbeattie to the hills beyond. These houses are the ones shown on the left of the previous picture.

Frazer & Young opened quarries in Rounall Wood to the north of Dalbeattie in the 1870s, largely as a test of the local stone. By 1880 they had moved across the hill to these working faces at Cow Park which were worked until 1950. In 1894 they installed an 80 tons per day crusher beside the railway yard at the station. This was very unpopular with the townsfolk because of the amount of dust it created which blew around the town in a northerly wind and especially over clothing that had been hung out to dry on a washing line!

Andrew Newall began prospecting for granite in the early nineteenth century and by the 1820s he owned several quarries in the area including this one at Craignair on the far side of the Urr. Dalbeattie granite was used to build many public works in England such as the lower part of the Eddystone Lighthouse, the Thames Embankment, Liverpool Docks and both Manchester and Birkenhead town halls, whilst many towns and cities are paved with setts and kerbs made from it. The setts had to be cut and shaped by hand and this picture shows several men at work on this task, sitting in their individual wooden huts that they could turn around according to the wind direction. Large insurance companies were especially fond of using granite for building their principal offices because it gave the appearance of rock-solid assurance; examples of such buildings can be seen in London, Liverpool and Leeds. A significant proportion of the quarries' output was exported, resulting in several public buildings and lighthouses in many parts of the world being constructed of this material. A later development was crushing smaller and misshapen stones to make products ranging from concrete and road metal to railway ballast and garden paths. A half-mile-long ropeway used to run from their crushing plant adjacent to the quarry down to a loading bank by the railway and around 200 tons per day of crushed granite could be transported in buckets along the ropeway. In 1907 Dalbeattie's two largest quarries between them produced 70,000 tons of granite each year and in 1916 the Rev C H Dick wrote that "Craignair is being gradually removed and distributed over the world". Nowadays this quarry at Craignair is the only one left working in the area. Its present-day owners are Tarmac Limited and its only product is crushed rock aggregate.

This picture dates from the early years of the twentieth century. Until 1841 the granite from Craignair Quarry had been used only for building purposes but in that year they began a polishing process for memorial stones and the like. This became so popular and widely-admired that Newalls exhibited a large stone with a Scotch thistle incised on it at the Great Exhibition of 1851.They offered several standard designs and this picture shows typical ones under construction. The firms of Newall and Shearer amalgamated and instituted a steam-powered polishing works in these buildings but, unfortunately for them, polished granite went out of fashion and the works closed down in the 1940s. The premises are now occupied by Jardine's Garages in Craignair Street.

PUBLIC SCHOOL, DALBEATTIE. 269/101.

The Dalbeattie School Board was set up in 1873 and on 5th May 1876 this school, designed by James Barbour of Dumfries, was opened in Southwick Road, replacing five existing small schools in the burgh. The Roman Catholics retained their own St Peter's school. For the first two years the headship was shared between Mr Davidson of the Established Church and Mr Thompson of the Free Church; they were paid equal salaries, had separate rooms and employed independent staffs. Davidson resigned in 1878 and Thompson in 1882, the latter in a dispute with the Board over his salary. The average attendance was 326 in 1876 and 645 in 1909. The site for the school cost £300 plus around a further £2,200 for the building. Initially called the Public School, it subsequently became the High School until it was replaced in 1958 by a new High School in Haugh Road, after which it became a primary school. The school building was enlarged in 1900, 1911, 1962 and 1980.

Dalbeattie used to have a substantial area of allotments situated just to the west of the High Street. The Urr Parish and Dalbeattie Horticultural Society, formed in 1896, held annual exhibitions at Haugh of Urr and Dalbeattie alternately. This picture is dated 1938 and shows the extensive and neat areas of cultivation in the town prior to the Second World War. After the war, interest in allotments declined, they were taken out of use and eventually the modern housing estate of McLellan Gardens was built on their site.

Dalbeattie Burn appears to have come into use for driving undershot mill wheels as early as the 1600s. Weirs across the burn channelled water into a lade that discharged into an impoundment (the Mill Dam, pictured here) north of the burn. In this picture the Munches Sawmill is on the left and the granite polishing works is in the stone building. The Mill Dam is now filled in as an overspill car park for local businesses and the local clinic.

A subscription and circulating library was instituted in Dalbeattie in 1851 and the following year it was decided to form a Mechanics Institute in connection with the library with Mr Maxwell of Munches as its first President. Meetings were initially held in the Town Hall but in 1911 this purpose-built Mechanics Institute was erected on a site at the Mill Isles near Craignair Street on land granted by Mr WHJ Maxwell of Munches. The building eventually outlived its original purpose and nowadays, with modern extensions, has become the Dalbeattie Health Centre.

The electricity works, formerly a forge and powered by the Dalbeattie Burn, was situated near the Sunnyside houses on Barrhill above Carswell's Mill and supplied electricity to the town at 110 volts. It is now a private house.

On 10th April 1901 Miss Eliza Mary Copland made a gift of one and a half acres of land for a parsonage to be built in Blair Road just behind Christ Church Episcopal Church. The building was completed in 1902 and was built of granite with a slate roof. Eventually it became too expensive for the church to maintain and in 1989 it was sold to a private buyer. This is a 1913 Christmas card view of the parsonage which is situated in an idyllic location and approached by a drive lined with mature trees. In more recent years its extensive grounds have been reduced by an estate of council houses having been built behind it further up the street at Craigmath.

This is the graceful bridge over the Urr at the end of Craignair Road that still carries the main road west from Dalbeattie to Castle Douglas. It was built in 1797 of stones brought from Kirkgunzeon because the local granite wasn't yet being exploited. In 1799 it was mentioned in Robert Heron's "Journey through Scotland" that there were a few cottages at the Craignair Bridge together with a dyeing house and a corn mill. This tranquil view is looking upstream in 1906; one would hardly guess that the huge Craignair Quarry is just out of sight beyond the left side of the bridge, hidden by the trees. Today the road is the busy A711 and traffic is controlled by traffic lights at each end of the bridge because it is too narrow to allow two vehicles to pass one another.

Glenlair House near Dalbeattie was the home of the famous scientist James Clerk Maxwell who was born in Edinburgh in 1831 but who lived at Glenlair for most of his life until his death in 1879. The house was largely destroyed by fire in 1929 and for many years remained a ruin. The oldest part of the house was restored in 1993 by the present owner, Captain Duncan Ferguson, for his mother's use but the principal restoration work on the house began on 31st March 2008. This started with the porch which has now been completely restored, helped by a donation of 10,000 euros from the European Microwave Association. Captain Duncan Ferguson has now established the "Maxwell at Glenlair" Trust to stabilize the building and set up a permanent monument to the scientist.

The well-preserved remains of the Mote of Urr stand impressively on the west bank of the Urr close to the B794 road between Haugh of Urr and Dalbeattie. Originally it was a great motte-and-bailey castle that was probably constructed in the mid-12th century for Walter de Berkeley, the King's Chamberlain. The bailey measures 152 metres by 66 metres and is surrounded by a fifteen metre wide ditch. Near its east end is a seven metre wide ditch around the motte which once stood about ten metres high. It is believed to have been occupied until around the 14th century.

The railway line west of Dumfries was originally single track. Doubling of the line started in 1876 and this viaduct over the Urr at Barsoles was built in 1880 by Messrs JBA M'Kinnell of Dumfries Foundry. It comprised a girder deck and guardrails set on four pairs of masonry columns across the river. This 1909 view is looking towards Castle Douglas with Buittle Station about ³/₄ mile further on. The line between Dumfries and Challoch Junction near Stranraer was closed on 14th June 1965 and the viaduct's steelwork was sold for scrap, but the masonry columns remain standing today.

Buittle Church lies off the A711 road a short distance from Dalbeattie in the direction of Castle Douglas. Designed by Walter Newall and built by John Graham of Castle Douglas in 1819, it was extended in 1902 by James Barbour of Dumfries who added a chancel and vestry on the south side. The gables of the ruins of the old Parish Church can be seen on the right. This was substantially a medieval church but was altered in the 16th and 17th centuries after the Reformation. The west (left hand) gable and various other parts of the church were rebuilt in 1743-45. The ruins are taller and more impressive than they look in the picture because they lie in a depression in the ground. A huge granite memorial to the Maxwell family of Munches stands in the churchyard.

Palnackie Village by Dalbeattie. 83

This view of Palnackie village around 1920 is looking down the length of Port Street towards the harbour. The parish hall on the left was built in 1877 by the Rev. James Robb Grant who was minister of the parish for forty-four years and who died in 1889. Apart from two windows in the roof its appearance is unchanged today. The white building next to it is the Glenisle Inn and the shop in the centre of the picture is Carswell's Grocers and Drapers. Subsequently the shop doorway has been sealed with stone blocks and the building is now a private house.

The two ladies in this early 1920s picture are standing in the doorway of what is nowadays the second house in Glen Road. Port Street runs across the picture down towards the harbour to the right and the end section of the Glenisle Inn is next to the small white building in the centre which has since been demolished to allow an extension to the Glenisle's bar and outdoor seating. The house in the centre of the picture used to be the Customs House. The row of houses on the left still looks almost the same; indeed, apart from a garage built onto the former Customs House and new windows and new paint everywhere, the whole view has hardly changed in almost ninety years.

Most of the older houses in the village such as these in Port Street are built of rubble stone which has then been painted. The left hand side of the building with steps leading up to the two front doors used to be the Royal Oak public house (its cellar doors can be seen to the left) whilst the post office occupied the right side; the postman wearing his uniform and peaked cap is standing by a post box let into the wall. The 1837 local directory shows that at that time they were both operated by Thomas Dalling. The building is now two private houses numbered 14 and 16 Port Street.